DATE DUE			

791.45
WHI

30408000003590
Whiting, Jim.

American idol judges

Woodland High School
Henry County Public Schools

428220 02295   29837D   0004

MODERN ROLE MODELS

American Idol Judges

Jim Whiting

WOODLAND HIGH SCHOOL
800 N. MOSELEY DRIVE
STOCKBRIDGE, GA 30281
(770) 389-2784

Mason Crest Publishers

Produced by OTTN Publishing in association with
21st Century Publishing and Communications, Inc.

MASON CREST PUBLISHERS INC.
370 Reed Road
Broomall, Pennsylvania 19008
(866) MCP-BOOK (toll free)
www.masoncrest.com

Printed in the United States of America.

First Printing

9 8 7 6 5 4 3 2 1

Library of Congress Cataloging-in-Publication Data

Whiting, Jim, 1943–
    American idol judges / Jim Whiting.
        p. cm.—(Modern role models)
    ISBN 978-1-4222-0496-2 (hardcover) — ISBN 978-1-4222-0783-3 (pbk.)
    1. American idol (Television program)—Juvenile literature. 2. Cowell, Simon,
1959–   —Juvenile literature. 3. Abdul, Paula—Juvenile literature. 4. Jackson,
Randy—Juvenile literature. I. Title.
    PN1992.77.A56W45 2008
    791.45'7—dc22   2008025385

Publisher's note:
All quotations in this book come from original sources, and contain the spelling
and grammatical inconsistencies of the original text.

CROSS-CURRENTS

In the ebb and flow of the currents of life we are each influenced
by many people, places, and events that we directly experience
or have learned about. Throughout the chapters of this book you
will come across CROSS-CURRENTS reference boxes. These
boxes direct you to a CROSS-CURRENTS section in the back
of the book that contains fascinating and informative sidebars
and related pictures. Go on. ▸▸

CONTENTS

(Clockwise, from left) Simon Cowell, Ryan Seacrest, Randy Jackson, and Paula Abdul. Ryan is the host of *American Idol*, and Simon, Randy, and Paula are the judges. Although viewers ultimately decide which pop star hopeful will win *American Idol*, the judges narrow the competition down to 24 semi-finalists and critique each performance.

1

America Loves American Idol

ON THE EVENING OF JANUARY 15, 2008, EAGER viewers tuned in to the Fox Network for the two-hour premiere of the seventh season of *American Idol*. The telecast drew more than 33 million people. That audience was several million more than the combined totals of the shows broadcast by the other major networks—CBS, NBC, and ABC—that night.

The program featured scenes from the show's auditions in Philadelphia. That city was one of seven regional sites where thousands of hopefuls had originally performed. Now the survivors from those sites faced a team of three judges.

Along with host Ryan Seacrest, these three judges—Randy Jackson, Paula Abdul, and Simon Cowell—had become some of the country's most famous and powerful media personalities. As journalist Andy Dehnart points out,

> **"**The judges have been the same judges since the first season, and without them, the show would collapse. . . . No other show has been able to create a judging panel quite like this one, and that's thanks to their distinct personalities and clear understanding of the job they were hired to do.**"**

➤ DISTINCT PERSONALITIES ◄

Randy, one of the country's best bass players and a longtime recording executive, provides the industry perspective. As he says:

> **"**From my days playing neighborhood block parties in Baton Rouge, Louisiana, and out-of-the-way jazz clubs across the country to producing and writing songs on Mariah Carey's . . . album, *Charmbracelet*, I know what it takes to succeed—and fail—in this business.**"**

Randy is always the first one to speak and uses his knowledge to provide an objective critique of the performance. He may also offer constructive criticism.

Paula, whose pop star past made her famous even before the show's first season, follows Randy and is the "den mother" of the show. She is the most supportive judge, trying to say something positive about each performance. As she notes:

CROSS-CURRENTS
To learn more about the life and career of the host of American Idol, read "Ryan Seacrest." Go to page 47. ▶▶

> **"**I have the toughest job out of all the judges, I do believe. The one who keeps the hopes and dreams alive. I have to find the good so they're able to exit the stage with dignity no matter what.**"**

Simon, who became notorious because of his harsh statements, has a simple explanation of his role:

> **"**I'm the honest one. . . . We set out to make a show that honestly reflects the music business. And trust me—the record industry is *not* nice.**"**

Even after seven seasons, Simon's blunt comments can still catch Paula and Randy off guard. The three judges sometimes disagree on whether a contestant's performance was good or bad. Typically, Paula tries to pay everyone a compliment, Simon does not refrain from criticism, and Randy is somewhere in between. Their amusing banter has become a staple of the show.

Simon is fully aware that many viewers dislike him, but he feels that his very rudeness is part of the reason so many people tune in. So is the interplay among the three judges as they bring their respective roles into play.

⇒ WHO GOES TO HOLLYWOOD? ⇐

During the season opener, Paula, Randy, and Simon began making decisions about who would go on to Hollywood for the show's second round.

Some obviously had no chance of advancing. A 39-year-old man (who would have been disqualified anyway because he was over the age limit) who sang about **abstinence** did not make the cut. A 16-year-old girl who played middle linebacker for her school team and wanted to get help for her wheelchair-bound grandmother was sent home because her voice wasn't good enough. A woman with a Princess Leia hairdo joined the outgoing parade.

Others fared much better. The sentimental favorite was 26-year-old Angela Martin, a wedding singer from Chicago. She hoped to win *American Idol* to help support her daughter, who suffered from a serious nerve disorder. Another young woman who had her ticket to Hollywood punched was Kristy Lee Cook of Selma, Oregon. She had sold one of her horses to make the trip to the audition. Brooke White of Van Nuys, California, was the third competitor to hang in for another round. They joined 26 others for the cross-country trek.

160 TO 24 TO 12

Similar scenes of performance, elimination, and success took place across the country in the weeks that followed, resulting in a talent pool of 160 Hollywood hopefuls. During telecasts on February 12 and 13, the three judges whittled the number down to 24. At that point, viewers became involved. Over the next three weeks, their votes pared the 24 contestants down to six males and six females.

Cook and White made the elite group. The others were David Archuleta, Jason Castro, David Cook, Chikezie Eze, David Hernandez, Michael Johns, Ramiele Malubay, Syesha Mercado, Amanda Overmyer, and Carly Smithson.

Speaking to Oprah Winfrey soon after these selections were made, Simon made a startling revelation about what had become the most popular television program in the United States:

> **"**I remember thinking, 'If this year is not better than last year, I think it's going to be over. I think [people] are going to lose interest. Then, as luck would have it, in my opinion, I think we've got more talent this year than we've ever had on any season.**"**

SIMON SAYS: DAVID'S THE FRONTRUNNER

He told Oprah that in his opinion, 17-year-old David Archuleta was the clear frontrunner:

David Archuleta (left) and David Cook, the final two contestants of *American Idol*'s seventh season, strike lighthearted poses as they arrive at the season finale on May 20, 2008. Although the final show was filled with suspense, the judges agreed that both Davids had the talent and stage presence to be stars.

" But don't rule out Brooke White, David Cook and Jason Castro. Any one of these guys could win. I think it's going to get very, very interesting. "

The voters largely agreed with him, passing Archuleta, Cook and Castro along with Syesha Mercado to the round of four. Two weeks later, Castro and Mercado were gone and the two Davids went head-to-head. On Wednesday evening, May 21, the nation learned the identity of the seventh American Idol.

As the manager of some of the world's top-selling musicians, Simon Fuller established himself as a major player in the British music scene during the 1990s. With Simon Cowell, Fuller developed the format for an interactive singing competition. In Britain, *Pop Idol* became a huge success. However, at first the promoters could not sell the idea in the United States.

2

From Rejection to Acceptance

IN 2001, WORKING WITH ENGLISH RECORD manager Simon Fuller, Simon Cowell had developed a show for British television called *Pop Idol*. But the two Simons had a much larger audience in mind: the United States. So before *Pop Idol* even began airing, the Brits came to Los Angeles to pitch their show to American networks.

They were brimming with confidence. *Pop Idol* had been an easy sell back home. But the Americans were not so quick to see the charm of the series. The Simons first approached UPN, a network they felt could use a big hit. They were confident they could supply one. As Simon Cowell recalled, the meeting

❝[W]as a complete disaster from start to finish. . . . I had been selected

CROSS-CURRENTS

To learn more about the life and career of American Idol co-creator Simon Fuller, read "The Other Simon." Go to page 48. ▶▶

11

to make the pitch, and I thought I had done a brilliant job. . . . When I finished speaking, there was a terrible silence. 🙳

The results were no better when they called on ABC. The meeting took place in a tiny room. The man who listened to Simon Cowell's pitch didn't even let him finish before turning him down. Their reception at the other networks was similar. The Simons returned home without a deal.

⇶ TRYING AGAIN ⇜

That fall, in Britain, the **debut** of *Pop Idol* was a smash hit. The two Simons hired a Hollywood talent agency to try again to sell the series to the American market. However, *Pop Idol*'s enormous success didn't make much difference. No one was interested.

Then they caught a break. A television executive named Elisabeth Murdoch was a huge fan of *Pop Idol*. Her father, Rupert Murdoch, owned many media companies, including the Fox Network. Trusting his daughter's judgment, he ordered Fox executives to buy the show even though they had rejected it earlier. They obeyed him.

CROSS-CURRENTS

Check out "Rupert Murdoch" to learn about the media mogul who took a chance on American Idol *in 2002. Go to page 49.* ▶▶

Fox had planned to hire only American judges. But after watching *Pop Idol*—which included Simon Cowell as a judge—executives at Fox wanted to include him as part of the show. At first Simon was hesitant. A friend convinced him otherwise:

❝You're going to regret it if you don't go. If the show is a hit without you, you're going to think you could have been part of that. And if it isn't a hit, you're going to think that you could have made the difference. 🙳

⇶ TOO MANY TIME ZONES ⇜

As the producers worked to develop the new show for the summer of 2002, a problem emerged that no one had foreseen. In Britain, the show aired in the early evening. After the singers performed, audience votes were phoned in. Then, just before the network signed off for the night, the hosts reappeared to announce the results.

This **format** worked because all of Britain is within one **time zone**. But the United States covers four time zones. Fox had only two hours available for the show each night. The live broadcast of the show would air at 8 P.M. Eastern Standard Time (EST). A taped version would air on the West Coast at 8 P.M. Pacific Standard Time (PST). However, because states on the East Coast are three time zones—and therefore, three hours—ahead of the West Coast, viewers in the western states would not be able to watch the show before the voting ended. Fox could not announce the results the following morning because the network didn't have a national morning show.

Simon Cowell was a judge on *Pop Idol* before crossing the Atlantic to become part of *American Idol*. At first, he did not want to make the move. But American viewers tuned in to see Simon's harsh but honest criticisms of the performers. Soon, *American Idol* was a major hit for the Fox network.

The show depended on the audience voting. There was only one solution: a results show the next evening. Because the show would air during the summer, a "down time" for original programming, the extra time slot could easily be made available. *American Idol* was a go.

There was one final hurdle. The three judges had not met each other. How would they get along? Would they mesh or would they clash? Simon met the other two judges just before the first audition, but there was no time to discuss the show. When the first contestant finished, Randy told him, "That was a little bit pitchy, but you were good, dog. I kind of liked it." Paula added, "I loved your audition and I admire your spirit."

⇒ SIMON SHOWS HIS RUDENESS ⇐

Simon cleared his throat. His words were about to make television history:

> **"I think that we have to tell the truth here, which is that this singer is just awful. Not only do you look terrible, but you sound terrible. You're never going to be a pop star in a million years."**

Thoroughly embarrassed, the contestant fled the stage. Paula was horrified that Simon had been so harsh. Things got no better with succeeding singers. To Simon, they were even worse—and he told them so.

During a break, Paula said that she wanted to quit the show. Simon responded,

> **"We're not being vicious on purpose. Both you and I know what the music industry is like, and we have promised the American audience that we're going to portray it honestly. You're out there because you're sweet, and I'm out there because I'm not. It's about striking a balance."**

This explanation was convincing. Paula didn't bolt.

⇒ AN INSTANT HIT ⇐

The premiere was the most-watched show on its successive evenings. It was evident that though many people claimed to hate Simon's

First-season performers gather for a group hug to congratulate Kelly Clarkson (center), shortly after she was revealed as the winner of the first *American Idol* program. An estimated 50 million people watched the season finale on October 5, 2002. The show that once could not find a network home had become a huge success.

rudeness, they were fascinated. Soon Americans began watching in greater numbers. They eventually voted Kelly Clarkson the first American Idol.

The show was a huge success, far greater than Fox executives had dared to imagine. From this point on, the show would become a vital element of Fox's regular programming. It would start soon after the New Year and continue through late spring.

As an *American Idol* judge, Simon Cowell is not afraid to tell contestants exactly what he thinks of them. Simon doesn't consider his harsh criticism unkind. In fact, the producer and talent scout has said his comments help aspiring singers learn what it really takes to succeed in the highly competitive music business.

Simon Cowell

SIMON COWELL'S CHARACTERISTIC RUDENESS began at an early age. One day, when he was just four, his mother was dressing up to go out. As part of her outfit, she put on a large white fur hat. She asked Simon, "Does Mummy look pretty?" Simon took one look at her hat and replied, "Mum, you look like a poodle."

Simon was born on October 7, 1959, in Brighton, England. His father Eric was a wealthy real estate developer and his mother Julie was a former ballet dancer. Simon spent his early years on his family's estate north of London, and he didn't take long to develop a reputation as a "bad boy."

⇒ BAD BEHAVIOR ⇐

Simon used screwdrivers to scratch his parents' records if he didn't like the singer. He began smoking and drinking when he was nine.

A few years later, he pulled a toy gun on a bus driver. To Simon, this was a joke. To the terrified driver who didn't know that he was the victim of a prank, it was something entirely different.

Simon took his bad boy attitude to school. He disliked the discipline, and his classes were boring to him. He was often kicked out.

In desperation, his parents sent him to boarding school. That didn't work either. Simon dropped out when he was seventeen. By now his life goals narrowed down to one: making money.

⇒ THE MAILROOM ⇐

But he was just a high school dropout with a bad reputation and no idea how he would make "*real* money." His father tried to set him up in several jobs, but Simon wasn't interested. Then his mother came to his rescue. She saw an advertisement for a job in the mailroom at EMI records and even filled out the application form.

It wasn't glamorous, but the man who hired Simon made it clear that he could work his way up. However, Simon's upward progress was slow, and patience was not one of his strong suits. After a year, he left EMI. Simon worked briefly at a few other jobs, returned to EMI, and by 1982, he had quit again. Feeling he had a special gift as a talent scout and producer, Simon and his former boss at EMI, Ellis Rich, formed their own company focusing on music publishing.

Simon quickly realized that he had made a mistake. The new company struggled. He also realized that he was more interested in recording than in publishing music. In 1985, Simon joined forces with artists' manager Iain Burton to form Fanfare Records. At about the same time he met Pete Waterman, a member of the songwriting and music production company Stock Aitken Waterman. He credits his friendship with Waterman with teaching him virtually everything he needed to know about music production.

⇒ SUCCESS AND FAILURE ⇐

With Waterman's help, Fanfare Records produced singer Sinitta Malone's music. Sinitta, Simon's girlfriend at the time, had several hits, and Simon began spending money freely, buying a house and an expensive sports car. Though the romantic relationship did not last, Cowell and Sinitta remained friends. But the romance wasn't the only thing that didn't last. Fanfare went bankrupt in 1989. As Simon says,

"I effectively lost everything. I had to move in with my parents. In hindsight, it was the best thing that happened in my life because I learned the value of money: not to borrow money and not to live beyond my means. . . . One thing that I have always been able to do is to own up to my mistakes and not blame others.**"**

Simon signs autographs at the National Television Awards on October 31, 2006, in London, England. Behind him is Sinitta Malone, Simon's former girlfriend. During the late 1980s, Simon helped to make Sinitta into a singing star in the United Kingdom. Although their romantic relationship ended, Simon and Sinitta have remained friends.

CROSS-CURRENTS

To find out more about the American Idol winner who Simon Cowell has said was the best, read "Kelly Clarkson." Go to page 49. ▶▶

Still determined to succeed, Simon began working for Arista Records. This company was part of BMG, one of the world's largest recording companies. He made music based on well-known television figures such as the Power Rangers, Teletubbies, and figures from the World Wrestling Federation. The people he worked with at Arista were horrified. None of these were "real" singers. Simon persisted, however. He later explained:

Being a famous talent executive and TV personality has its benefits. Simon takes pride in his collection of luxury cars, including this Rolls Royce. His life today is very different from when he was a frustrated mailroom worker and aspiring music scout. Today, his net worth is estimated at more than $200 million.

❝My attitude was simple. I don't care what we're selling, as long as we're selling records. And those records went on to sell millions.❞

He soon moved on to RCA, another BMG label. He continued to be successful, in large part because he recognized—long before most other people in the music business—that there was a key link between television and music. Up to that point, nearly everyone believed that the key to selling records was radio airtime.

➤ ROBSON AND JEROME ◄

He used this knowledge in 1995 to make music stars of actors Robson Green and Jerome Flynn, who sang "Unchained Melody" during an episode of their TV series. At first the two men weren't interested in making a record. Simon was insistent. He called so often that Green threatened legal action. In the end, Simon won them over. "Unchained Melody" shot to the top of the charts in the U.K. Two number-one albums quickly followed. Simon was ecstatic:

❝I still look back on that period as one of the best times of my life. It was innocent and exciting and a very personal success. We went against the prevailing wisdom, made us all millions, and made an absolute fortune for BMG.❞

Starting in 1998, Simon made another fortune with the boy band Westlife. The group has sold more than 40 million records worldwide.

In 2001 he and Simon Fuller came up with the concept for *Pop Idol.* Simon Cowell had come a long way from the EMI mailroom—but not so far from the little boy who told his mother she looked like a poodle.

In the 2003 children's DVD *Zoe's Dance Moves*, Paula Abdul teaches a simple dance routine to *Sesame Street* Muppets and their young fans. Long before *American Idol*, Paula was a professional dancer and pop singer, and planned dance routines for other performers. Her musical experience made her a candidate for the role of an *American Idol* judge.

Paula Abdul

PAULA ABDUL WAS BORN IN SAN FERNANDO, California, on June 19, 1963. Her father Harry owned a sand and gravel company and once worked as a livestock trader. Lorraine, her mother, was a former assistant to movie director Billy Wilder and also a one-time concert pianist. Paula joined an older sister, Wendy.

It didn't take Paula long to find her direction in life. As she recalled,

> **❝I was four years old sitting on the couch with my parents watching *Singin' in the Rain* on TV. I was just watching Gene Kelly have a great time and I can remember looking at my parents in the living room and saying, 'I want to do that.'❞**

Most children would have moved on to other interests. Not Paula. She kept watching old musicals and wanting to do what she was seeing.

⇒ ON STAGE ⇐

Her parents' divorce in 1969 may have accelerated the process. Her mother wanted Paula to do something that made her happy and knew that meant show business. So when she was seven, Paula began appearing with local theater groups. She was so good that she was asked to **choreograph** a musical when she was in junior high.

Her success continued at Van Nuys High School. In addition to acting and dancing in school plays, she was also a cheerleader. By the time she graduated, she knew she wanted a career as a performer.

Her mother wanted Paula to go to college, just in case her dancing career didn't take off. She had a point: Paula stands just five feet, two inches tall—several inches shorter than most professional dancers. So Paula enrolled at California State College at Northridge.

During her freshman year, a friend suggested she try out for the Los Angeles Lakers dance team. When she saw hundreds of tall young women at the audition, Paula nearly chickened out. But she decided to give it her best shot.

⇒ A LAKER GIRL ⇐

Her courage was rewarded. She was one of 12 women who were chosen to form the dance team. Within a few months she became the group's choreographer. As she said,

> **❝It was the perfect outlet to experiment with different ideas that I had. I was this cheerleader who kind of broke the rules. I wanted to get rid of the pom-pom thing and focus more on dance.❞**

Within two seasons, other eyes became focused on Paula. They belonged to the Jackson brothers, who had achieved fame as the Jackson Five. The Jacksons needed a choreographer for "Torture," a single from their 1984 *Victory* album. That led to a job working with Janet Jackson, the family's youngest member, who was finally emerging as a solo performer. Soon other performers were clamoring to work with Paula.

But Paula wanted to do more than help other people dance well. She wanted to sing and dance herself. She spent thousands of dollars to create a **demo tape**. Virgin Records signed her to a contract.

Paula smiles for the camera at the 1990 Emmy Awards. In the late 1980s and early 1990s, she became a bestselling singer as well as a choreographer for movies and music videos. However, she took a long break from Hollywood to deal with career and health issues. Joining the *American Idol* judges' panel threw Paula back into the spotlight.

⇛ SUCCESS . . . AND PROBLEMS ⇚

Paula's first album, *Forever Your Girl*, was released in June 1988. At first it didn't do very well. But the third single, "Straight Up," shot to the top of the charts. This helped the album to eventually sell more than 10 million copies.

Her success continued in 1991 with her second album, *Spellbound*. Coupling her singing with her music videos, Paula had become a pop music superstar. But not everything was going her way. She married actor Emilio Estevez in 1992, but they split up two years later.

CROSS-CURRENTS

To learn more about the life and career of one of American Idol's most successful contestants, read "Clay Aiken." Go to page 50. ▶▶

A failed marriage wasn't Paula's only problem. She had suffered from **bulimia** for many years. Paula was a perfectionist who was obsessed with her height and weight. This obsession led to the bouts of secret overeating and purging that characterize the disease. Fortunately, Paula managed to free herself from this cycle. She later said,

❝Conquering [bulimia] back in 1994, to me, was a crowning moment, more than having number one records.❞

Paula supports a variety of humanitarian and charitable causes, including child health, animal rights, and environmental protection. As a National Eating Disorders Association spokesperson, Paula shares the story of her struggle with bulimia to help prevent eating disorders. She is signing this poster to endorse a product that boosts fuel efficiency when used in cars.

Her courage in going public prompted the National Eating Disorders Association to ask her to serve as a celebrity spokeswoman.

In 1996 Paula married clothing executive Brad Beckerman. The marriage lasted for just 17 months. Her professional life was also showing some strains. *Head Over Heels*, her third album, didn't sell well. She left Virgin and took a **hiatus** from the music business.

⇒ LIVING WITH CONSTANT PAIN ⇐

One reason for the break, which she kept to herself, was severe physical pain, dating back to an injury she suffered in high school. The intense demands of dancing only made things worse. As she explained,

> **"It's something that is so aggressive that it takes your breath away and makes your teeth start chattering because it's so uncomfortable. They gave me pills that would put a 300 pound man out. And there were no answers."**

She would eventually undergo 10 surgeries and lose an inch in height in a search for relief.

⇒ STILL GOING ⇐

Nevertheless, Paula continued her choreography, working on such hit movies as *Jerry Maguire* and *American Beauty*. She also appeared in guest star roles on television shows.

Despite her separation from Virgin Records, the company released *Paula Abdul: Greatest Hits* in 2000. Sales were poor. Paula was drifting even further from the mainstream of public awareness. But her former success led to an invitation to join *American Idol*. She didn't take the opportunity for granted:

> **"I count my blessings when I sit down in that seat and I wait for the contestants to get out there. I can't wait to let them see my excitement. You only dream of roles like this. I'm living my role in life."**

Before becoming a judge on *American Idol*, Randy Jackson spent more than 20 years working in the music industry. During the 1980s, he was in constant demand as a studio bassist and keyboard player. He also toured with the rock group Journey, and worked as a songwriter, music producer, and talent scout.

5

Randy Jackson

RANDY JACKSON WAS BORN IN BATON ROUGE,
Louisiana, on June 23, 1956. His father Herman worked as a foreman
for the Exxon oil company, while his mother Julia was a homemaker.
Influenced by his older brother Herman Jr., a drummer, Randy
began playing several instruments at an early age. These included the
saxophone, piano, guitar, bass, and drums.

A key moment in Randy's development came one evening
when he was 14. Big Bo Melvin & the Nighthawks, a local group,
were rehearsing on bass player Sammy Thorton's front porch.
Randy recalls,

> **"Sammy turned me on my head. He was an
> incredible player, just a natural."**

Randy began taking lessons from Thorton and quickly became a
fixture in his school orchestra and citywide groups. He also played
with John Fred and His Playboy Band, which had once scored a
national number-one hit with the song "Judy in Disguise [With
Glasses]." Randy received a scholarship to study briefly in Los Angeles

with Chuck Rainey, who would eventually become the most recorded bass player in music history.

➤ PLAYING WITH LEGENDS ◆

After high school, Randy attended Southern University in Louisiana. He graduated from Southern in 1979 with a Bachelor of Arts degree with a double major in music and psychology. During his college years he joined famous jazz drummer Billy Cobham's band, playing on two of Cobham's albums and beginning his career as a studio musician. Randy would later credit his time with Cobham, as well as playing with John Fred, as playing a crucial role in his development:

> **When you play with people that are that legendary, everyone goes, 'Wow, this guy can really play because Billy wouldn't have no slouch. . . . I guess this guy's really good because John Fred can have whoever he wants in his band and he's got this guy.' It's the company you keep.**

During this time he married singer/songwriter Elizabeth Jackson, and the couple had a daughter, Taylor.

➤ MAKING HIS WAY ◆

During the 1980s, Randy Jackson became well known within the music industry as a talented professional bass and keyboard musician. He worked as a musician for studio recording sessions. His reputation for versatility grew, and he was nicknamed "The Emperor" for his skill and talent in all types of music, especially jazz, rhythm and blues, and pop. He would eventually appear on more than a thousand albums. These included records by dozens of well-known artists such as Madonna, Aretha Franklin, Elton John, Whitney Houston, Celine Dion, George Michael, and Bruce Springsteen.

In 1983 Randy got his first "big break" as a live performer when two members of the band Journey quit. Randy was one of four musicians hired to replace them, serving as a long-term guest bassist. His stint had a significant effect on his development. As he explained,

> **The Journey guys are progressive rock musicians who were ahead of their time, like Toto. They had a**

As a college student, Randy honed his musical talent by playing with award-winning jazz drummer Billy Cobham (pictured). Since the late 1960s, Cobham has collaborated with other well-known musicians, including trumpet player Miles Davis and guitarist Carlos Santana. Cobham's music is known as jazz fusion, because he combines jazz with elements of other musical genres, like funk or soul.

no-holds-barred rule, artistically; they would come up with interesting chord changes and arrangements. That's why their music is, and always will be, around. From my time there, I learned the real rock & roll experience and the fact that something can be great art and still be wildly commercial. **99**

⇒ CHANGES IN THE AIR ⇐

Randy took what he had learned into the next phase of his career, which began early in the 1990s. While continuing to record with many of the industry's biggest names, he branched out into the production end of the business and also found himself in demand as a songwriter. Through his work as a producer, Randy rose to the high-powered position of vice president of Artists and Repertoire (A&R) at Columbia Records.

Randy poses with Morris the cat, mascot for 9Lives cat food, at the 2006 launch of Morris' Million Cat Rescue Campaign. Since its creation, the drive has helped over 1 million homeless cats find new owners. Randy also volunteers his time for organizations that fight child poverty and health problems, including Save the Children and obesity prevention groups.

His personal life also underwent major changes during this time. He and Elizabeth divorced in 1990, and Randy married former ballet dancer Erika Riker in 1995. Erika and Randy are parents of two children, Zoe and Jordan.

With his career as a musician well established and his career as a producer in full swing, Randy moved to a higher position as senior vice president of Artists and Repertoire at MCA Records.

By early 2002, Randy Jackson had spent more than 20 years as a professional musician and record producer. Randy had no idea he was about to embark on a new career as one of the most well-known television personalities in America. He was originally unenthusiastic about the concept behind *American Idol*. After seeing several episodes of the show's British forerunner, *Pop Idol*, however, Randy decided to give it a chance. He would bring his A&R experience searching for new talent into a new television venue that offered young and talented singers a chance at stardom.

CROSS-CURRENTS

The *American Idol concept* has spread to other countries. Read "Foreign Idol" to find out more. Go to page 51. ▶▶

From Simon Cowell's standpoint, Randy's presence on the show rounded out the personality circle. Randy made an immediate and very strong impression:

> **❝'Sunny' didn't even begin to describe him—he could light up any room, no matter what the size—but without being irritating. . . . He was familiar with the show, understood the concept, and on top of all that he was entirely qualified. ❞**

People in the music industry had long been familiar with these qualities. Now Randy was about to reveal them on a national stage.

But Randy says the show's success is not about him, or about the other judges, for that matter:

> **❝It's the *Rocky* story in it. We're out to find the best undiscovered [talent] and really herald that. ❞**

And that's exactly what the *American Idol* judges have done.

AMERICA
WHO'S NEXT?

American Idol

Each new season of *American Idol* is accompanied by tremendous excitement from the viewing public. Before Simon, Paula, and Randy select the finalists, each season's first episodes are devoted to preliminary auditions, which guarantee a mixture of good, mediocre, and bizarre performances. In its first seven seasons, *American Idol* has become a television institution.

6

Becoming Must-See TV

AFTER THE FIRST SEASON OF *AMERICAN IDOL*, Fox executives realized that the network had a huge hit on its hands. Fox immediately prepared for a second season. Because *American Idol* would now be part of the network's regular lineup, auditions had to begin within a few weeks after Clarkson was named the winner of season one, on September 4, 2002.

In Simon's mind, it was very important that Kelly Clarkson's single "A Moment Like This" had to sell well. He later explained,

> **"If the single had stiffed after six months of hard work on the television series, we would have lost a tremendous amount of credibility for future seasons. We had to prove to the people who were**

watching that *American Idol* wasn't just a talent show but the gateway to a real career. **"**

There was no guarantee that "A Moment Like This" would be a hit. At that time, the music market in the United States was sluggish. However, the song entered the charts at number 52, and within a week it had climbed to the top spot. It was the biggest jump in *Billboard* chart history. Eventually the record would sell more than a million copies. Simon could finally relax.

➤ No Change in Judges ⬅

The first show of the second season aired on January 21, 2003. The judging panel—one of the primary reasons for the show's success—remained intact. However, season one co-host Brian Dunkleman didn't return. Ryan Seacrest became the sole announcer, a post he has maintained ever since.

On the final show, Ruben Studdard edged out Clay Aiken for the top spot in the closest vote ever. Over time, however, Aiken would prove to be the more successful performer in terms of record sales. Much less successful was *From Justin to Kelly*, a movie about season one winner Kelly Clarkson and runner-up Justin Guarini. It was released a month after the second season ended, but flopped.

Simon took advantage of his high public profile that year to publish his book *I Don't Mean to be Rude, But . . .: Backstage Gossip From American Idol & the Secrets That Can Make You a Star*. At the end of the book he **distilled** the things he had learned from more than two decades in the record industry into a single word: determination. The best-known entertainers move beyond their comfort zone because they have the determination to go as far as they can. In terms of the show, he explained:

"When people get turned down by us on *American Idol*, some of them look deflated, like it's the end of the world. I would like to see some of them resurface a year later, or three years later, with a new image, a better sense of their talent, and a career. It would be inspiring to me if some of the *American Idol* losers became stars of the same **magnitude** as the winners. It would speak to their focus and ambition. **"**

Kelly Clarkson (center) received a Platinum Award for selling 1 million copies of her debut album *Thankful*, which included her first single, "A Moment Like This." Presenting the award were (left to right) RCA Music Group vice president Steve Ferrera, RCA president and CEO Clive Davis, Simon Fuller, and RCA chief operating officer Charles Goldstuck.

☀ OUTSIDE OF *AMERICAN IDOL* ☀

When the second season ended, Simon was able to complete a project he had begun two years earlier. He formed a vocal quartet called Il Divo, which means "divine performer." It consists of four handsome and very stylish men in their 30s from four different countries, who perform pop classics in operatic style in several different languages.

The group released its first album, *Il Divo*, the following year. The album reached the top of the charts in 13 countries. Since then the group has released two more albums. Total sales of the three albums are estimated at more than 15 million.

Simon also sold his share of S Records, a company he had established to market the winners of *Pop Idol*, and made more than

Simon, Randy, and Paula pose with Ryan Seacrest (center). For many *American Idol* viewers, much of the show's appeal comes from watching undiscovered singers develop into polished performers. Because Simon, Paula, and Randy offer feedback on every performance, they contribute not only to the show's dynamic, but also to the contestants' artistic growth.

$40 million. But not everything he touched turned to gold. He produced the matchmaking show *Cupid*, which debuted during the summer of 2003. The show received poor ratings and was quickly canceled.

In 2003, Randy underwent **gastric bypass surgery** to lose weight. Randy, who weighed nearly 350 pounds, needed to slim down because he had been diagnosed with diabetes the previous year. Diabetes is a disease that affects a person's energy level and has serious long-term effects, including blindness, nerve damage, and heart disease. Many people with diabetes are able to control the disease by living a healthier lifestyle and reducing their weight. The gastric bypass surgery was somewhat risky, with a 2 percent chance that Randy wouldn't survive. The procedure was successful, however, and within a short time Randy had lost about 100 pounds.

Randy also followed Simon into the publishing world. His book *What's Up Dawg?: How to Become a Superstar in the Music Business* came out in 2004.

⟫ SEASON THREE SUCCESSES ⟪

During the third season of *American Idol*, in 2004, Fantasia Barrino emerged victorious in balloting that exceeded the combined totals of the first two seasons. But another big winner that season was Jennifer Hudson. Although Jennifer was eliminated midway through the final round, her singing had attracted major attention. She eventually joined the cast of the 2006 film *Dreamgirls*, and won an Academy Award as Best Supporting Actress.

One "highlight" of the early episodes of season three was William Hung, an engineering student at the University of California at Berkeley. He became almost certainly the show's most famous non-qualifier. Hung's screechy rendition of Ricky Martin's hit "She Bangs" caused Paula and Randy to turn away and laugh. Simon said,

CROSS-CURRENTS

Read "Jennifer Hudson and Dreamgirls" to learn about an American Idol contestant who has become a star. Go to page 52. ▶▶

> **"You can't sing, you can't dance, so what do you want me to say?"**

Many contestants would have argued with Simon. But Hung simply said,

> **"I already gave my best and I have no regrets at all."**

Perhaps because of his humble response and recognition of his obvious limitations, almost overnight Hung became a media celebrity. He appeared on talk shows, had parts in several movies, and released three albums—and achieved much more lasting name recognition than many singers who have made the show's final rounds.

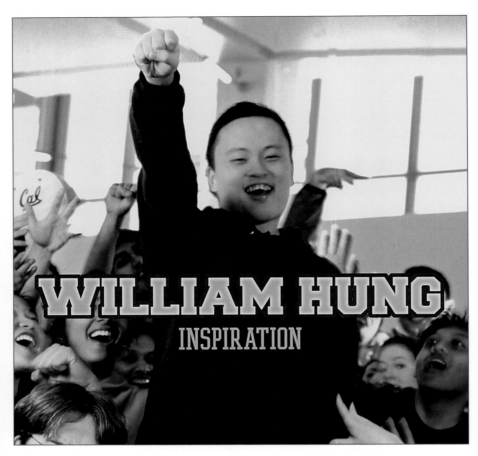

The cover of third-season contestant William Hung's debut album, *Inspiration*. The novelty album featured Hung's version of "She Bangs," which made a lasting impression on the *American Idol* judges—and on the show's viewers. Unlike most *Idol* hopefuls who don't make it past the audition stage, William Hung became a celebrity after his brief appearance on the show in 2004.

⇒ A RUNAWAY WINNER ⇐

Country singer Carrie Underwood was the winner in 2005. Simon had predicted her triumph, and viewers agreed. *American Idol* officials later said that they didn't make the vote totals public each week, because Underwood's margin of victory was usually so large they were afraid people would lose interest in the show.

As season four neared the end, former contestant Corey Clark—who had been disqualified several years earlier for not revealing that he had a police record—claimed that Paula had coached him and had an inappropriate relationship with him. Fox investigated and decided that there wasn't any evidence that she had done anything wrong.

CROSS-CURRENTS

To learn more about one of the most successful American Idol winners, check out "Carrie Underwood." Go to page 54. ▶▶

That wasn't the only negative situation that swirled around Paula. For some time, tabloid and internet stories about her odd behavior had led to rumors of drug or alcohol abuse. She explained that she had suffered from chronic pain, and it had caused the odd behavior. Medication soon brought the situation under control. Once again, Fox fully supported Paula.

The top 24 finalists of season four pose for a publicity photo. On May 25, 2005, Carrie Underwood (far left, wearing the blue shirt) was named the winner. During its fourth season, *American Idol* experimented with format changes so the show's now-established formula wouldn't bore viewers. For example, guest judges occasionally appeared with Simon, Randy, and Paula.

➤ SEASONS FIVE AND SIX ➤

Taylor Hicks was the winner in 2006, though Chris Daughtry—who soon formed the rock band Daughtry—has been more successful commercially. Daughtry's first album sold more than 3 million copies.

Just before Valentine's Day 2006, Paula made an appearance on the Dr. Phil show, asking for hints about looking for love. She also spoke publicly about being Jewish—her father is a Syrian Jew and her mother is a Canadian Jew—and announced plans to visit Israel.

Simon put the failure of *Cupid* behind him as he produced two successful shows: *American Inventor* and *America's Got Talent*. In 2006 he received a substantial raise for agreeing to do five more seasons

Although Chris Daughtry (second from left) finished in fourth place on *American Idol*'s fifth season, the show gave him the exposure he needed to make his band Daughtry a success. The band's self-titled debut album was Billboard's top-selling album of 2007. Chris has also collaborated with popular rock acts like Live, Bon Jovi, and Matchbox Twenty.

of American Idol. He was already making a reported $8 million a year, and wouldn't divulge the amount of the new contract. Some estimates pegged the figure at $25 million annually, or even higher.

In 2007, Jordin Sparks defeated Blake Lewis in a finale that set a new record for votes. The season also featured the saga of Sanjaya Malakar, who survived for several weeks as a finalist even though the judges didn't think much of him.

Paula's run of bad luck continued when she broke her nose just before the 2007 show's finale. It didn't stop her from appearing, however. On a happier note, she debuted a line of jewelry on the shopping network QVC that did very well.

➣ "IDOL GIVES BACK" ⬿

A highlight of 2007 was the production of "Idol Gives Back" in April. The show included video of Paula, Randy, and Simon visiting poverty-stricken sites in Africa and the United States. The combined efforts of dozens of big-name entertainers helped to raise more than $75 million to alleviate hunger and disease. Simon recognized that this funding would go a long way to help African children:

> **❝The amazing thing . . . is how little money you need to save a life. I mean it's not thousands of dollars. It's something like a dollar. So [diseases like malaria] can be eradicated like that [snapping his fingers]. Very easy to get rid of, and that should not exist today.❞**

For Simon and the others, "Idol Gives Back" was far from their only charitable venture. Simon contributes to a number of organizations that help children in poverty, the environment, and animals. Early in 2008 he announced that he would donate $180 million to several charities in his will.

The other judges are also very involved in charity work. Jackson is active in Morris' Million Cat Rescue (from which he got his own cat, Dawg), the American Heart Association, Save the Children, The Ronald McDonald House, NARAS Music for Schools, and other organizations.

Charities that Paula supports besides the National Eating Disorders Association include Clothes Off Our Back, In Defense of Animals, Leeza's Place, Peace Alliance, and The Rescue Train.

Simon reads a book with students in Kenya. The school he visited was profiled on the first "Idol Gives Back" broadcast, which aired April 25, 2007. Charitable donations from the "Idol Gives Back" shows are used to address problems that affect the world's poorest people: hunger, inadequate health care, poor sanitation, and limited access to education.

SEASON SEVEN SURPRISES

In March 2008, during the seventh season of *American Idol*, the album *Randy Jackson's Music Club, Vol. 1* was released. Randy had produced all of the songs. The first single from the album was by his fellow judge Paula. "Dance Like There's No Tomorrow" put her back on the *Billboard* 100 chart for the first time in nearly 12 years. She released a new album of original material a few months later.

A second "Idol Gives Back" show was aired April 9, 2008. Once again, many stars joined the *American Idol* contestants to raise more than $60 million for children's charities in Africa and the United States.

The seventh season finale was held at the Nokia Theatre in Los Angeles. The two finalists, David Cook and David Archuleta, each sang three songs. The judges praised both singers, though Simon earned a cascade of boos from the audience when he suggested that David Cook's final song rated just six and a half out of a possible ten.

Paula didn't share Simon's opinion, and she gave Cook a one-woman standing ovation. Randy, on the other hand, seemed to go along with Simon. As always, Simon had the last word. He had earlier given Archuleta the nod in the first two rounds. Now, he said,

> **"You came out here tonight to win, and what we have witnessed is a knockout."**

Simon was half right. The audience had indeed witnessed a knockout. But it belonged to Cook, who swamped Archuleta by a margin of more than 12 million votes from the record-breaking 97.5 million votes cast via phone and text messaging.

Simon may have had an inkling of that outcome. Just before the announcement of Cook's victory, he did something he had almost never done before. He apologized to Cook, saying that his comments the night before verged on disrespect:

> **"When I went back home and watched it, it wasn't quite so clear cut as we called it."**

⟫ THE MOST POWERFUL SHOW ⟪

In 2008, for the fifth year in a row, *American Idol* was the highest-rated prime-time television show. It was the major reason Fox became the most popular American network for the first time since Rupert Murdoch had created the network in the mid-1980s. Most people agreed with an article in *Rolling Stone* magazine that said,

> **_American Idol_ is the most powerful show in TV history. . . . No other program has come close.**

The three judges have all spoken about how much they enjoy being part of *American Idol*. As Randy Jackson said about the final episode of the show's second season,

American Idol remains one of the most popular television programs in the United States. Each week, about 30 million people tune in to watch this showcase for amateur talent. It has inspired movies, other television shows, and even video games. Many of the top performers on *American Idol* have gone on to achieve remarkable successes in the music industry.

> **❝**I felt like a proud parent. In a cheesy, sentimental, corny way, I felt I had done something good in the world: I helped somebody with amazing talent get their shot at the big time because they deserved it. Yo, now that's the way you get down.**❞**

It's likely that Simon, Paula, and Randy will continue helping many other young singers to "get down" as the show continues in upcoming seasons.

Ryan Seacrest

From an early age, Ryan Seacrest knew he wanted a career in broadcasting. Born in a suburb of Atlanta, Georgia, on Christmas Eve in 1974, Seacrest didn't waste any time pursuing his ambition. He made morning PA announcements while he was in high school, worked on the student newspaper, and participated on the debate team.

When he was 16, he began an **internship** with an Atlanta radio station and soon made his first on-air broadcast. By the time he was in his early twenties he had moved to Los Angeles, where he branched into television and also hosted the afternoon show on Star 98.7, a leading Los Angeles radio station.

Along with Brian Dunkleman, he was named to co-host *American Idol* in 2002. When Dunkleman left after the season's end, Ryan became the sole host and the public face of the show.

Radio Gigs

Ryan used his new national fame to launch a new television program in 2004, *On Air with Ryan Seacrest*, which folded after nine months. By then he had landed two prime radio gigs. One was replacing the legendary Casey Kasem on the weekly program *American Top 40*. He also took over the morning drive program on KIIS-FM, the top-rated show in Los Angeles in its time slot.

He received his own star on the Hollywood Walk of Fame the following April. That summer, he was named as executive producer and host of the television program *Dick Clark's New Year's Rockin' Eve* and announced that he would succeed Clark when the legendary rock music figure retired.

In 2007, he introduced his clothing company, the R Line. He had a small role in the hit movie *Knocked Up*. By that time he also owned several restaurants.

Be Careful What You Wish For

Ryan appreciates all of his success, but he also knows that his fame is the result of much hard work. As he told newspaper reporter Patricia Sheridan,

> **"I had dreams of just being able to afford a house with a yard like I grew up in, which wasn't that big of a house. I remember thinking to myself every night when I would get home from school, 'How's my Dad paying for the bills?' And thinking, 'I just want to do a job where I don't have to work as many hours as my Dad.' Of course, now I think I work twice as many a day."**

(Go back to page 6.)

The "Other" Simon

Mention "Simon" in conjunction with *American Idol*, and everyone assumes you're talking about Simon Cowell. But another Simon—Simon Fuller—played a vital role in the show's success. He set up the show's format, first in the United Kingdom and then the United States.

Born in 1960 in Hastings, England, Fuller became interested in the music business when he began booking bands for dances at his college. In 1981, he worked for Chrysalis Records and promoted "Holiday," Madonna's first big hit. Four years later, he helped propel Paul Hardcastle's song "19" to sales of more than 3 million copies. Its success led him to found his first company, 19 Entertainment.

Simon Fuller's 19 Entertainment has managed singers such as Annie Lennox, the Spice Girls, and Amy Winehouse. In 2005, he created the TV show *So You Think You Can Dance*. He helped sign soccer superstar David Beckham to a five-year, $250 million contract with the Los Angeles Galaxy in 2007. He also became involved in fashion and interior design.

In 2007, *Time* magazine named Simon Fuller one of the world's 100 most influential people. The following year, the Producers Guild of American gave him its Visionary Award. The group also praised him for his charity work.

(Go back to page 11.)

American Idol *co-creator Simon Fuller (right) poses on the set of the first "Idol Gives Back" program, April 25, 2007. Fuller has played an important role in the program's success. Also there to celebrate is movie director Richard Curtis, who founded an annual British charity telethon featuring celebrities. Simon Fuller used this telethon as a model for "Idol Gives Back."*

Rupert Murdoch

Rupert Murdoch was born in 1931 in Melbourne, Australia. His father was an important newspaper publisher. Murdoch went to England to attend college and begin his journalism career. He returned to Australia in 1953 when his father died and left him one of his father's newspapers.

He began buying other newspapers in Australia and used them to support politicians who shared his conservative beliefs. In 1964 he began *The Australian*, a newspaper similar to *USA Today*. Four years later he expanded his operations to include the United Kingdom when he bought *The News of the World*, the world's most popular English-language paper. He soon bought other large British newspapers.

Murdoch came to the United States in 1973 when he bought the *San Antonio Express-News*. Soon afterward he founded *The Star*, a supermarket tabloid, and purchased the *New York Post* in 1976. In 1985 he created the Fox Network. Because U.S. law prohibits foreigners from owning TV stations, he became a U.S. citizen. A decade later Murdoch established the Fox News Channel, one of the country's leading sources of broadcast news. He bought the *Wall Street Journal* in 2007.

Today Rupert Murdoch is one of the world's most powerful media executives. His net worth is estimated at several billion dollars.

(Go back to page 12.)

Kelly Clarkson

Kelly Clarkson was born in Burleson, Texas, in 1982. When Kelly was 13 and in middle school, a teacher heard her singing in the hall and encouraged her to join the school choir. Her talent quickly developed. When she graduated from high school, she made some demo tapes and headed to Los Angeles.

Like many others before her, Kelly failed to hit it big in LA and moved back home. Not long afterward, though, a friend told her about the *American Idol* auditions. Kelly decided to enter, and she immediately stamped herself as a favorite with her rendition of the Aretha Franklin hit "Respect."

After winning the competition with nearly 60 percent of the votes in the finals, she signed a recording contract. Her first single, "A Moment Like This," debuted at number 52 on the *Billboard* charts. The next week, the song reached the top spot, setting a "leap to number one" record. The Beatles had set the previous mark in 1962, when "Can't Buy Me Love" jumped 26 spots to reach number 1.

Since then Kelly has released three albums, all of which have done very well, and established a solid career. In a 2008 interview, Simon Cowell said that she had the best voice of the six winners to that point.

(Go back to page 20.)

Clay Aiken

Born in 1978 in Raleigh, North Carolina, Clay Aiken discovered his singing talent at a young age. He joined several singing groups and also acted in school musicals. When he graduated from high school, he entered the University of North Carolina at Charlotte and majored in special education.

Diane Bubel, the mother of an autistic boy whom Clay had been assisting, encouraged him to try out for *American Idol*. After some initial success, he was dropped from the competition. But he returned for the wild card round, where he sang well enough to become a finalist. The show's producers also suggested a makeover to make him more appealing. He replaced his glasses with contacts and adopted a spiky hairstyle.

In the finals, Clay placed second to Ruben Studdard in the closest vote in *American Idol* history. Finishing second didn't hurt his career at all. He has released four albums, gone on eight tours, written a book, made numerous television appearances and appeared on Broadway for the first time in 2008 in the musical *Spamalot*.

As a UNICEF ambassador, Clay Aiken spent Christmas of 2007 in Chiapas, Mexico. He visited a shelter for children left homeless by flooding. Before Clay competed on American Idol, he taught autistic students in special education classes. Now, he uses his fame to connect with children in need and to draw attention to their problems.

Clay has also been active in charity work. He founded the Bubel/Aiken Foundation to help children with **autism** and has been involved in a number of programs for UNICEF.

(Go back to page 26.)

Foreign Idols

American Idol is broadcast in more than 100 countries, some of which wait days or even weeks to view each episode. And given the show's worldwide popularity, it's not surprising that more than 40 countries—spanning every continent except Antarctica—have adopted their own version of the show. Though each country gives the show a slightly different name, the basic **format** remains the same.

These countries include Austria (*Starmania*); China (*Super Girl*, a show for females only); Ethiopia (*Ethiopian Idols*); Germany (*Star Search*); Israel (*A Star Is Born*); Philippines (*Search for the Star in a Million*); Singapore (*Project SuperStar*); and Turkey (*Oriental Star*).

Broadcast from Lebanon, *Superstar* is one of the oldest and broadest-based versions of *American Idol*. It encompasses virtually the entire Arab world. Entrants reflect the pride of their respective countries and in many cases attract votes because of their nationality rather than their ability.

Among the most interesting of these national versions is *Afghan Star*, which debuted in Afghanistan in the fall of 2005 and declared its first winner early the following year. Until 2001, Afghanistan had been ruled by the Taliban, Islamic fundamentalists who enforced strict religious laws. The Taliban had outlawed pop music and other elements of American culture. Even today, some elements of the population strongly disapprove of the show because it represents a foreign influence. But most Afghans appear to like *Afghan Star* and what it symbolizes about their country's striving for modernization. The show has undergone a steady increase in popularity among the viewing audience. More than 2,000 entrants tried out for the show's third season, in which a woman placed third.

In 2003, a *World Idol* competition held in England included Kelly Clarkson from the United States and winners from 10 countries that had their own *Idol* shows. Each country also supplied a judge. Simon Cowell was the representative of the United States for his participation on *American Idol*.

Viewers from the 11 countries were the only ones allowed to vote, and they couldn't vote for the person from their own country. Kurt Nilsen of Norway was the winner, with Clarkson second and Peter Evrard of Belgium third.

Another *World Idol* competition is tentatively scheduled for 2010. It will be held in the United States.

The worldwide popularity of *American Idol* led to *American Dreamz*, a 2006 movie that was a **parody** of the show. It starred Hugh Grant, Dennis Quaid, and Mandy Moore.

(Go back to page 33.)

Jennifer Hudson and *Dreamgirls*

Born on September 12, 1981, in Chicago, Jennifer began singing in gospel choirs when she was seven. Even though she had little formal voice training, she spent several months with Disney Cruise Lines. When she was selected to compete on *American Idol* during 2004, she quickly became one of the judges' favorites.

But viewers were less enthusiastic about Jennifer than the judges. She finished in the bottom three during the first two episodes and was gone for good after the sixth. It seemed likely that she would lapse back into obscurity.

In 2005, Jennifer managed to score an audition for the film version of *Dreamgirls*, a musical loosely based on the history of the popular 1960s group The Supremes. So did 782 other singers—one of them Fantasia Barrino, who had won *American Idol* in 2004. To her own astonishment, Jennifer was cast as Effie, in the film's most important role.

A Near Miss

Jennifer almost missed out on the role. When the original group had been narrowed to 20, each young woman took a screen test. No one connected with the film was impressed with Jennifer, except writer/director Bill Condon. On Condon's recommendation, she was chosen for the part.

There were other obstacles. Audiences had completely identified with Jennifer Holliday, who had played Effie in the original Broadway production, especially the way she sang the show's most important song, "And I'm Telling You (I'm Not Going)." In addition, Jennifer Hudson was an unknown who would be acting with megastars like Beyoncé Knowles, Jamie Foxx, Danny Glover, and Eddie Murphy. Finally, Effie and Jennifer had completely different personalities. This untested actor would really have to act.

Meeting All Challenges

Jennifer came through on all counts, singing, dancing, and acting. Critics and audiences alike were blown away by her performance of "And I'm Telling You (I'm Not Going)." She swept major awards for Best Supporting Actress: the Golden Globes, Screen Actors Guild, and—most important—the Academy Awards. She became one of a handful of actors to receive an Oscar for her debut performance.

The Oscar put her on a fast track to stardom. In March 2007, she became the third African-American woman to appear on the cover of *Vogue* magazine. The first two were Oprah Winfrey and Halle Berry. Jennifer may be destined for the same level of fame. She appeared in two movies in 2008—*Sex and the City* and *Winged Creatures*—and began work on a third. Her debut album was scheduled for release late that year.

(Go back to page 32.) ◀◀

At first, soft-spoken Jennifer Hudson had a difficult time portraying hot-tempered Effie, her character in Dreamgirls. Jennifer was ordered to practice being bossy around the set. She also had to gain 20 pounds for the role. Jennifer's hard work paid off, as her performance won an Academy Award for Best Supporting Actress.

Carrie Underwood

Carrie Underwood was born in 1983, and grew up on her parents' farm in Checotah, Oklahoma. From an early age, her talent was apparent. She sang in school productions and community functions. She was ready to stop singing when she graduated from high school, however. She felt she had to be practical. She majored in broadcast journalism at Oklahoma's Northeastern State University, planning a career in TV news.

Carrie's **sorority** sisters encouraged her to keep singing. She followed their advice. Then she read about the tryouts for *American Idol*. At first she was reluctant. Then her mother offered to drive her to St. Louis for the tryouts.

Even winning the title and starting a recording and concert career didn't keep Carrie from completing her college education in 2006. The following year, she became the first *American Idol* winner to sweep the top three national awards: American Music, Billboard, and Grammys.

Many people say Carrie's success is due largely to her being so natural. She remains down to earth and willing to give to others. In 2006, she toured Iraq and Kuwait to entertain U.S. troops. She is also active in the Humane Society of the United States.

(Go back to page 40.) ◀◀

Carrie Underwood signs an autograph before the 2005 Country Music Awards program. Carrie is among the most successful American Idol *winners. Her first two albums, 2005's* Some Hearts *and 2007's* Carnival Ride, *have sold over 10 million copies. Carrie has also won three Grammy Awards and 13 Billboard Music Awards.*

1956 Randy Jackson is born on June 23 in Baton Rouge, Louisiana.

1959 Simon Cowell is born on October 7 in Brighton, England.

1963 Paula Abdul is born on June 19 in San Fernando, California.

1976 Simon drops out of school.

1979 Randy graduates from Southern University; Simon gets a job in the mailroom at EMI records.

1981 Paula graduates from Van Nuys High School with a 3.85 grade point average.

1982 Paula is selected as a Laker Girl and soon becomes the group's choreographer.

1983 Randy joins the rock band Journey.

1985 Simon sets up Fanfare Records to market Sinitta Malone's single "So Macho."

1989 Fanfare Records goes bankrupt and Simon moves back with his parents for a brief period.

1990 Randy divorces wife Elizabeth.

1992 Paula marries Emilio Estevez.

1994 Paula reveals that she has struggled with bulimia since high school; Paula and Emilio Estevez divorce in May.

1995 Randy marries Erika Riker; Simon produces "Unchained Melody" by Robson and Jerome, which becomes a number-one hit in the United Kingdom.

1996 Paula marries Brad Beckerman; they would divorce in 1998.

2001 Simon Cowell and Simon Fuller debut *Pop Idol* in England.

2002 Paula, Randy, and Simon become judges on *American Idol*.

2003 Randy undergoes gastric bypass surgery and loses more than 100 pounds; Simon publishes *I Don't Mean to Be Rude, But . . .*

2004 Simon appears on an episode of *The Simpsons*, in which he judges babies applying for a pre-nursery school; Randy publishes *What's Up Dawg?: How to Become a Superstar in the Music Business*.

2006 Randy and Morris the Cat join forces to begin Morris' Million Cat Rescue Campaign to find homes for a million homeless cats; Simon produces the television programs *American Inventor* and *America's Got Talent*.

2007 Paula, Randy, and Simon help "Idol Gives Back" earn more than $75 million.

2008 Paula releases the single "Dance Like There's No Tomorrow," which is included on Randy's album *Randy Jackson's Musical Club, Vol. 1*; in addition to the album, Randy produces the show *America's Favorite Dance Crew* for MTV; Simon donates $162,000 to the family of a girl suffering from cancer.

PAULA ABDUL

Albums

1987   *Forever Your Girl*

1991   *Spellbound*

1995   *Head Over Heels*

2000   *Paula Abdul: Greatest Hits*

Singles

1989   "Knocked Out"
"(It's Just) The Way That You Love Me"
"Straight Up"
"Forever Your Girl"
"Cold Hearted"

1991   "Rush Rush"
"Promise of a New Day"

1992   "Blowing Kisses in the Wind"
"Will You Marry Me?"
"Vibeology"

1995   "My Love Is For Real"
"Crazy Cool"

1996   "Ain't Never Gonna Give You Up"

2008   "Dance Like There's No Tomorrow"

Awards and Honors

1989   Emmy, Outstanding Achievement in Choreography for *The Tracey Ullman Show*

1990   Emmy, Outstanding Achievement in Choreography for *The 17th Annual American Music Awards*

1991   Receives star on the Hollywood Walk of Fame

2005   Receives Profiles in Living Award from the National Eating Disorders Association

RANDY JACKSON

Albums
2008   *Randy Jackson's Musical Club, Vol. 1*

Awards and Honors
2008   Named Save the Children's first-ever United States Programs Ambassador

SIMON COWELL

Awards and Honors
2003   Teen Choice Award–Favorite TV Personality

2003   Number 33 on British Channel 4's list of 100 Worst Britons We Love to Hate

2004   Teen Choice Award–Choice Reality/Variety Jackass

Books

Carter, Bill. *Desperate Networks*. New York: Doubleday, 2006.

Catalano, Grace. *Paula Abdul: Forever Yours*. New York: Penguin Books, 1990.

Cowell, Simon. *I Don't Mean To Be Rude, But . . .* New York: Broadway Books, 2003.

Cowell, Tony. *I Hate To Be Rude, Bu . . .: Simon Cowell's Book of Nasty Comments*. London: John Blake Publishing, 2006.

Jackson, Randy. *What's Up, Dawg? How to Become a Superstar in the Music Business. With K.C. Baker*. New York: Hyperion, 2004.

Lawlor, Michelle. *Kelly Clarkson*. Broomall, Penn.: Mason Crest, 2007.

Tracy, Kathleen. *Clay Aiken: From Second Place to the Top of the Charts*. Hockessin, Del.: Mitchell Lane, 2004.

Web Sites

http://www.paulaabdul.com/
Paula Abdul's official Web site includes her bio, photos, and a newsletter.

http://www.ryanseacrest.com
Ryan Seacrest's official Web site, with news, links, updates, photos, and newsletter.

http://www.americanidol.com/
The official Web site for American Idol carries continually updated news, features, photographs, recaps of shows, videos of performances, and information on previous seasons.

http://www.biggeststars.com/r/randy-jackson-home.html
An unofficial site for Randy Jackson, with a biography, photo gallery, news, and links to other sites.

http://www.tv.com/simon-cowell/person/104611/summary.html
This Web site includes a biography of Simon Cowell, along with quotes, facts, and links to related sites.

abstinence—to refrain from having sex.

autism—condition in which it is difficult to have normal social relationships and communicate with others.

bulimia—condition characterized by overeating and then intentionally vomiting what has just been eaten.

choreograph—to plan out and arrange the steps that dancers will take along with a certain song.

debut—first appearance.

demo tape—a recording designed to show a singer's talent to a record producer.

distilled—summarized.

eradicated—wiped out.

format—way of organizing material.

gastric bypass surgery—operation that reduces the size the stomach and allows food to bypass part of the small intestine, making a person feel full faster and absorbing fewer calories into the body.

hiatus—a break from a certain kind of activity.

internship—opportunity for a person with little experience in a certain field to work in that field for a period of time and gain practical experience, usually for little or no money.

magnitude—size, extent.

parody—a work of art that imitates a well-known work and makes fun of it.

sorority—a social organization for women, usually based at a college or university.

time zone—any of the 24 areas (running north-south) into which the world is divided, and within which the same standard time is used.

page 6 "The judges have been . . ." Andy Dehnart, "'Idol' judges have grown into their roles," MSNBC (January 17, 2007). http://www.msnbc.msn.com/id/16548080/

page 6 "From my days..." Randy Jackson with K.C. Baker, *What's Up, Dawg? How to Become a Superstar in the Music Business* (New York: Hyperion, 2004), p. 4.

page 6 "I have the toughest job . . ." Erik Hedegaard, "Idol Worship," *Rolling Stone* (April 6, 2006), p. 50.

page 6 "I'm the honest one . . ." Simon Cowell, *I Don't Mean to Be Rude, But . . .* (New York: Broadway Books, 2003), p. 2.

page 8 "I remember thinking . . ." "Simon Cowell's Discoveries," *The Oprah Winfrey Show* (March 17, 2008).

page 9 "But don't rule out . . ." "Simon Cowell's Discoveries," *The Oprah Winfrey Show* (March 17, 2008).

page 11 "was a complete disaster . . ." Cowell, *I Don't Mean to Be Rude, But . . .*, p. 93.

page 12 "You're going to regret it . . ." Bill Carter, *Desperate Networks* (New York: Doubleday, 2006), pp. 186–187.

page 14 "I think that we have . . ." Cowell, *I Don't Mean to Be Rude, But . . .*, 106–107.

page 14 "We're not being vicious . . ." Cowell, *I Don't Mean to Be Rude, But . . .*, p. 108.

page 17 "Does Mummy look pretty?" Cowell, *I Don't Mean to Be Rude, But . . .*, p. 14–15.

page 18 "*real* money . . ." Cowell, *I Don't Mean to Be Rude, But . . .*, p. 30.

page 19 "I effectively lost everything . . ." Stacy Perman: From Idol to Inventor," *Business Week* (January 31, 2006). http://www.businessweek.com/smallbiz/content/jan2006/sb20060130_727793.htm

page 21 "My attitude was simple . . ." Hedegaard, "Idol Worship," p. 50.

page 21 "I still look back . . ." Cowell, *Rude*, 80.

page 23 "I was four years old . . ." Grace Catalano, *Paul Abdul* (New York: Signet, 1990), p. 16.

page 24 "It was the perfect outlet . . ." Catalano, *Paula Abdul*, p. 30.

page 26 "Conquering [bulimia] back in 1994 . . ." Ann Curry, "Paula Abdul's second act: 'American Idol' judge knows what it takes to reach the top," NBC News (Dec. 9, 2003). http://www.msnbc.msn.com/id/3080040/

page 27 "It's something that is so . . ." Curry, "Paula Abdul's second act."

page 27 "I count my blessings . . ." Curry, "Paula Abdul's second act."

page 29 "Sammy turned me on my head . . ." Chris Jisi, "Randy Jackson! The Big Bass Story of a True American Idol," *Bass Player* (March 2008). http://www.bassplayer.com/article/randy-jackson/march-08/34265

page 30 "When you play with people . . ." Associated Press, "Randy Jackson is ready for his close-up," MSNBC (Jan. 31, 2005). http://www.msnbc.msn.com/id/6890979/

page 30 "The Journey Guys . . ." Jisi, "Randy Jackson!"

page 33 "'Sunny' didn't even begin . . ." Cowell, *I Don't Mean to Be Rude, But . . .*, p. 103.

page 33 "It's the *Rocky* story . . ." Tracey Ford, "Randy Jackson Feels 'Idol,'" *Rolling Stone* (Feb. 3, 2006). http://www.rollingstone.com/news/story/9231668/randy_jackson_feels_idol

page 35 "If the single had stiffed . . ." Cowell, *I Don't Mean to Be Rude, But* . . . , p. 141.

page 36 "When people get turned down . . ." Cowell, *I Don't Mean to Be Rude, But* . . . , p. 240-241.

page 39 "You can't sing . . ." Associated Press, "The 'Idol' star who can't sing," CNN (Feb. 23, 2004). http://www.cnn.com/2004/SHOWBIZ/Music/02/23/music.idoldreamer.ap/index.html

page 39 "I already gave my best . . ." Associated Press, "The 'Idol' star who can't sing," CNN (Feb. 23, 2004). http://www.cnn.com/2004/SHOWBIZ/Music/02/23/music.idoldreamer.ap/index.html

page 43 "The amazing thing . . ." Christopher Rocchio, "Simon Cowell discusses importance of 'Idol Gives Back' charity event," *Reality TV World*, April 24, 2007. http://www.realitytvworld.com/news/simon-cowell-discusses-importance-of-idol-gives-back-charity-event-5061.php

page 45 "You came out here tonight . . ." Lynn Elber, "In 'Idol' bout, 'Archie' declared knockout winner," Associated Press (May 21, 2008). http://ap.google.com/article/ALeqM5iwXD4BoO2HF6nbttn2FU7Cw_ZtowD90PT5V80

page 45 "When I went back home . . ." Timothy Finn, "Cook becomes more than hometown Idol," *Kansas City Star*, May 22, 2008. http://www.kansascity.com/826/story/630660.html

page 45 "American Idol is the most . . ." Hedegaard, "Idol Worship," p. 48.

page 46 "I felt like a proud parent . . ." Jackson, *What's Up, Dawg*, p. 222–223.

page 47 "I had dreams of just . . ." Patricia Sheridan, "Ryan Seacrest," *Pittsburgh Post Gazette* (Dec. 25, 2006). http://www.post-gazette.com/pg/06359/748293-129.stm

Jim Whiting has written more than 100 children's non-fiction books and edited well over 150 more during an especially diverse writing career. He published *Northwest Runner* magazine for more than 17 years. His other credits include advising a national award-winning high school newspaper, sports editor for the *Bainbridge Island Review*, event and venue write-ups and photography for American Online, articles in dozens of magazines, light verse in the *Saturday Evening Post*, the first piece of original fiction to appear in *Runner's World*, and official photographer for the 1999 Antarctica Marathon.

PICTURE CREDITS

page

1: Fox Network/NMI
4: Fox Network/NMI
7: Fox Network/KRT
9: Fitzroy Barrett/Landov/MCT
10: 19 Entertainment/NMI
13: BMG/PRMS
15: Splash News
16: Fox Network/KRT
19: CoolPotoDudes/CIC Photos
20: Zuma Press
22: Sony Wonder/NMI
25: Mirrorpix Photos
26: Ethos Environmental/NMI
28: American Heart Asso./FPS

31: Adil BSU/NMI
32: Del Monte Foods/NMI
34: Fox Network/KRT
37: RCA Records/NMI
38: Fox Network/NMI
40: Kock Records/NMI
41: Fox Network/NMI
42: 19 Recordings/PRMS
44: Fox Network/PRMS
46: CIC Photos
48: 19 Entertainment/NMI
50: U.S. Fund for UNICEF/NMI
53: Kaye Evans-Lutterodt/NMI
54: Kodak/Business Wire/PRMS

Front cover: Fox Network/KRT